WE

THE HUMANS

ABHILASH CHAUBEY

Contents

Preface   v

1. Homo Sapiens   1

2. Defination   8

3. Biology   18

4. Psychology   31

5. Culture And Society   39

6. The Sun   50

7. The Earth   60

Preface

This book is a basic encyclopedia on Humans, The sun and The Earth.

CHAPTER ONE

Homo Sapiens

Humans (Homo sapiens) are the most abundant and widespread species of primate, characterized by bipedalism and large, complex brains. This has enabled the development of advanced tools, culture, and language. Humans are highly social and tend to live in complex social structures composed of many cooperating and competing groups, from families and kinship networks to political states. Social interactions between humans have established a wide variety of values, social norms, and rituals, which bolster human society. Curiosity and the human desire to understand and influence the environment and to explain and manipulate phenomena have motivated humanity's development of science, philosophy, mythology, religion, and other fields of study.

Although some scientists equate the term humans with all members of the genus Homo, in common usage it generally refers to Homo sapiens, the only extant member. Anatomically modern humans emerged around 300,000 years ago in Africa, evolving from Homo heidelbergensis or a similar species and migrating out of Africa, gradually replacing local populations of archaic humans. For most of history, all humans were nomadic hunter-gatherers. Humans began exhibiting behavioral modernity about 1

0,000- 0,000 years ago. The Neolithic Revolution, which began in Southwest Asia around 13,000 years ago (and separately in a few other places), saw the emergence of agriculture and permanent human settlement. As populations became larger and denser, forms of governance developed within and between communities and a number of civilizations have risen and fallen. Humans have continued to expand, with a global population of over 7.9 billion as of 2022.

Genes and the environment influence human biological variation in visible characteristics, physiology, disease susceptibility, mental abilities, body size and life span. Though humans vary in many traits (such as genetic predispositions and physical features), any two humans are at least 99% genetically similar. Humans are sexually dimorphic: generally, men have greater body strength and women have a higher body fat percentage. At puberty, humans develop secondary sex characteristics. Women are capable of pregnancy, and undergo menopause and become infertile at around the age of 50.

Humans are omnivorous, capable of consuming a wide variety of plant and animal material, and have used fire and other forms of heat to prepare and cook food since the time of H. erectus. They can survive for up to eight weeks without food, and three or four days without water. Humans are generally diurnal, sleeping on average seven to nine hours per day. Childbirth is dangerous, with a high risk of complications and death. Often, both the mother and the father provide care for their children, who are helpless at birth.

Humans have a large and highly developed prefrontal cortex, the region of the brain associated with higher cognition. They are intelligent, capable of episodic memory, have flexible facial expressions, self-awareness and a theory of mind. The human mind is capable of introspection, private thought, imagination, volition and forming views on existence. This has allowed great technological advancements and complex tool development possible through reason and the transmission of knowledge to subsequent generations. Language, art and trade are defining characteristics of humans. Long-distance trade routes might have led to cultural explosions and resource distribution that gave humans an advantage over other similar species.

Kingdom : Animalia

Phylum: Chordata

Class: Mammalia

Order: Primates

Suborder: Haplorhini

Infraorder: Simiiformes

Family: Hominidae

Tribe: Hominini

Genus: Homo,

Species: H. sapiens

Human Population

Etimology and Defination

All modern humans are classified into the species Homo sapiens, coined by Carl Linnaeus in his 1735 work Systema Naturae. The generic name "Homo" is a learned 18th-century derivation from Latin homō, which refers to humans of either sex. The word human can refer to all members of the Homo genus, although in common usage it generally just refers to Homo sapiens, the only extant species. The name "Homo sapiens" means 'wise man' or 'knowledgeable man'. There is disagreement if certain extinct members of the genus, namely Neanderthals, should be included as a separate species of humans or as a subspecies of H. sapiens.[4]

Human is a loanword of Middle English from Old French humain, ultimately from Latin hūmānus, the adjectival form of homō ('man' — in the sense of humankind).[7] The native English term man can refer to the species generally (a synonym for humanity) as well as to human males. It may also refer to individuals of either sex, though this form is less common in contemporary English.[8]

Despite the fact that the word animal is colloquially used as an antonym for human,[9] and contrary to a common biological misconception, humans are animals.[10] The word person is often used interchangeably with human, but philosophical debate exists as to whether personhood applies to all humans or all sentient beings, and further if one can lose personhood (such as by going into a persistent vegetative state).

Evolution

Humans are apes (superfamily Hominoidea).[12] The lineage of apes that eventually gave rise to humans first split from gibbons (family Hylobatidae) and orangutans (genus Pongo), then gorillas (genus Gorilla), and finally, chimpanzees and bonobos (genus Pan). The last split, between the human and chimpanzee–bonobo lineages, took place around 8–4 million years ago, in the late Miocene epoch.[13][14][15] During this split, chromosome 2 was formed from the joining of two other chromosomes, leaving humans with only 23 pairs of chromosomes, compared to 24 for the other apes.[16] Following their split with chimpanzees and bonobos, the hominins diversified into many species and at least two distinct genera. All but one of these lineages—representing the genus Homo and its sole extant species Homo sapiens—are now extinct.[17]

The genus Homo evolved from Australopithecus.[18][19] Though fossils from the transition are scarce, the earliest members of Homo share several key traits with Australopithecus.[20][21] The earliest record of Homo is the 2.8 million-year-old specimen LD 350-1 from Ethiopia, and the earliest named species are Homo habilis and Homo rudolfensis which evolved by 2.3 million years ago.[21] H. erectus (the African variant is sometimes called H. ergaster) evolved 2 million years ago and was the first archaic human species to leave Africa and disperse across Eurasia.[22] H. erectus also was the first to evolve a characteristically human body plan. Homo sapiens emerged in Africa around 300,000 years ago from a species commonly designated as either H. heidelbergensis or H. rhodesiensis, the descendants of H. erectus that remained in Africa.[23] H. sapiens migrated out of the continent, gradually replacing local populations of archaic humans.[24][25][26] Humans began exhibiting behavioral modernity about 160,000-70,000 years ago,[27] and possibly earlier.[28]

The "out of Africa" migration took place in at least two waves, the first around 130,000 to 100,000 years ago, the second (Southern Dispersal) around 70,000 to 50,000 years ago.[29][30] H. sapiens proceeded to colonize all the continents and larger islands, arriving in Eurasia 60,000 years ago,[31][32] Australia around 65,000 years ago,[33] the Americas around 15,000 years ago, and remote islands such as Hawaii, Easter Island, Madagascar, and New Zealand between the years 300 and 1280 CE.[34][35]

Human evolution was not a simple linear or branched progression but involved interbreeding between related species.[36][37][38] Genomic research has shown that hybridization between substantially diverged lineages was common in human evolution.[39] DNA evidence suggests that several genes of Neanderthal origin are present among all non sub-Saharan African populations, and Neanderthals and other hominins, such as Denisovans, may have contributed up to 6% of their genome to present-day non sub-Saharan African humans.[36][40][41]

Human evolution is characterized by a number of morphological, developmental, physiological, and behavioral changes that have taken place since the split between the last common ancestor of humans and chimpanzees. The most significant of these adaptations are obligate bipedalism, increased brain size and decreased sexual dimorphism (neoteny). The relationship between all these changes is the subject of ongoing debate.[42]

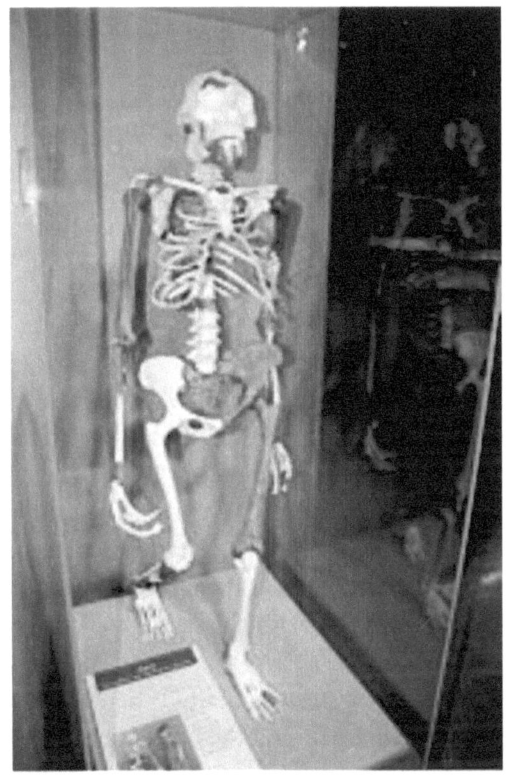

Reconstruction of Lucy, the first Australopithecus

CHAPTER TWO

Defination

History of Human Being

Until about 12,000 years ago, all humans lived as hunter-gatherers.[43][44] The Neolithic Revolution (the invention of agriculture) first took place in Southwest Asia and spread through large parts of the Old World over the following millennia.[45] It also occurred independently in Mesoamerica (about 6,000 years ago),[46] China,[47][48] Papua New Guinea,[49] and the Sahel and West Savanna regions of Africa.[50][51][52] Access to food surplus led to the formation of permanent human settlements, the domestication of animals and the use of metal tools for the first time in history. Agriculture and sedentary lifestyle led to the emergence of early civilizations.[53][54][55]

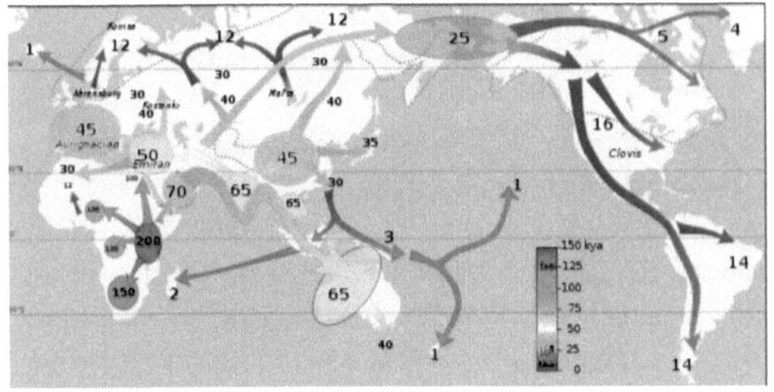

Overview map of the peopling of the world by early human migration during the upper paleolithic, following to the southern dispersal paradigm.

An urban revolution took place in the 4th millennium BCE with the development of city-states, particularly Sumerian cities located in Mesopotamia.[56] It was in these cities that the earliest known form of writing, cuneiform script, appeared around 3000 BCE.[57] Other major civilizations to develop around this time were Ancient Egypt and the Indus Valley Civilization.[58] They eventually traded with each other and invented technology such as wheels, plows and sails.[59][60][61][62] Astronomy and mathematics were also developed and the Great Pyramid of Giza was built.[63][64][65] There is evidence of a severe drought lasting about a hundred years that may have caused the decline of these civilizations,[66] with new ones appearing in the aftermath. Babylonians came to dominate Mesopotamia while others,[67] such as Poverty Point cultures, Minoans and the Shang dynasty, rose to prominence in new areas.[68][69][70] The Bronze Age suddenly collapsed around 1200 BCE, resulting in the disappearance of a number of civilizations and the beginning of the Greek Dark Ages.[71][72] During this period iron started replacing bronze, leading to the Iron Age.[73]

In the 5th century BCE, history started being recorded as a discipline, which provided a much clearer picture of life at the time.[74] Between the 8th and 6th century BCE, Europe entered the classical antiquity age, a period when ancient Greece and ancient Rome flourished.[75][76] Around this time other civilizations also came to prominence. The Maya civilization started to build cities and create complex calendars.[77][78] In Africa, the Kingdom of Aksum overtook the declining Kingdom of Kush and facilitated trade between India and the Mediterranean.[79] In West Asia, the Achaemenid Empire's system of centralized governance became the precursor to many later empires,[80] while the Gupta Empire in India and the Han dynasty in China have been described as golden ages in their respective regions.[81][82]

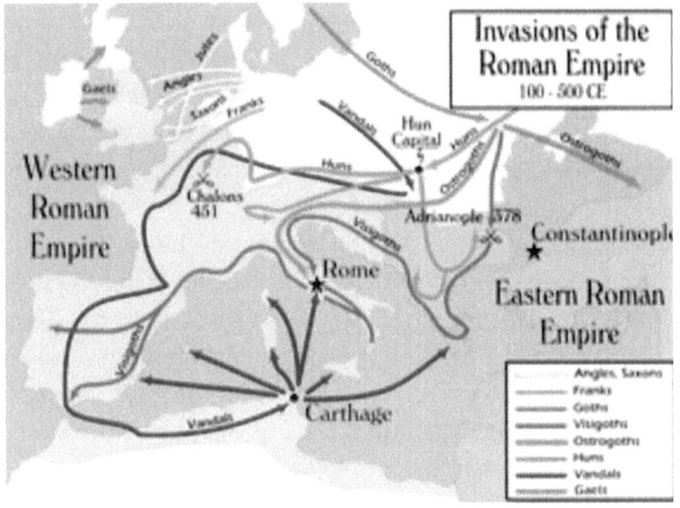

Enter Caption

Following the fall of the Western Roman Empire in 476, Europe entered the Middle Ages.[83] During this period, Christianity and the Church would provide centralized authority and education.[84] In the Middle East, Islam became the prominent religion and expanded into North Africa. It led to an Islamic Golden Age, inspiring achievements in architecture, the revival of old advances in science and technology, and the formation of a distinct way of life.[85][86] The Christian and Islamic worlds would eventually clash, with the Kingdom of England, the Kingdom of France and the Holy Roman Empire declaring a series of holy wars to regain control of the Holy Land from Muslims.[87] In the Americas, complex Mississippian societies would arise starting around 800 CE,[88] while further south, the Aztecs and Incas would become the dominant powers.[89] The Mongol Empire would conquer much of Eurasia in the 13th and 14th centuries.[90] Over this same time period, the Mali Empire in Africa grew to be the largest empire on the continent, stretching from Senegambia to Ivory Coast.[91] Oceania would see the rise of the Tu'i Tonga Empire which expanded across many islands in the South Pacific.[92]

Throughout the early modern period (1500–1800), the Ottomans controlled the lands around the Mediterranean Basin,[93] Japan entered the Edo period,[94] the Qing dynasty rose in China[95] and the Mughal Empire ruled much of India.[96] Europe underwent the Renaissance, starting in the 15th century,[97] and the Age of Discovery began with the exploring and colonizing of new regions.[98] This includes the British Empire expanding to become the world's largest empire[99] and the colonization of the Americas.[100] This expansion led to the Atlantic slave trade[101] and the genocide of Native American peoples.[102] This period also marked the Scientific Revolution, with great advances in mathematics, mechanics, astronomy and physiology.[103]

The late modern period (1800–present) saw the Technological and Industrial Revolution bring such discoveries as imaging technology, major innovations in transport and energy development.[104] The United States of America underwent great change, going from a small group of colonies to one of the global superpowers.[105] The Napoleonic Wars raged through Europe in the early 1800s,[106] Spain lost most of its New World colonies[107] and Europeans continued expansion into Oceania[108] and Africa (where European control went from 10% to almost 90% in less than 50 years).[109] A tenuous balance of power among European nations collapsed in 1914 with the outbreak of the First World War, one of the deadliest conflicts in history.[110] In the 1930s, a worldwide economic crisis led to the rise of authoritarian regimes and a Second World War, involving almost all the world's countries.[111] Following its conclusion in 1945, the Cold War between the USSR and the United States saw a struggle for global influence, including a nuclear arms race and a space race.[112][113] The current Information Age sees the world becoming increasingly globalized and interconnected.[114]

Habitat and Population

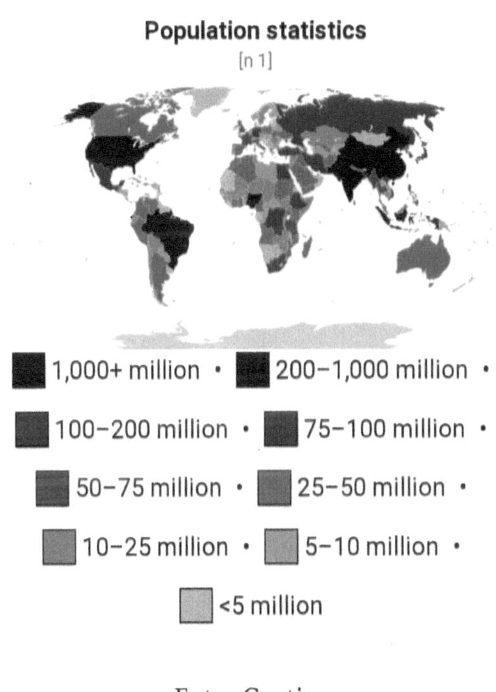

Enter Caption

Early human settlements were dependent on proximity to water and—depending on the lifestyle—other natural resources used for subsistence, such as populations of animal prey for hunting and arable land for growing crops and grazing livestock.[118] Modern humans, however, have a great capacity for altering their habitats by means of technology, irrigation, urban planning, construction, deforestation and desertification.[119] Human settlements continue to be vulnerable to natural disasters, especially those placed in hazardous locations and with low quality of construction.[120] Grouping and deliberate habitat alteration is often done with the goals of providing protection, accumulating comforts or material wealth, expanding the available food, improving aesthetics, increasing knowledge or enhancing the exchange of resources.[121]

Humans are one of the most adaptable species, despite having a low or narrow tolerance for many of the earth's extreme environments.[122] Through advanced tools, humans have been able to extend their tolerance to a wide variety of temperatures, humidity, and altitudes.[122] As a result, humans are a cosmopolitan species found in almost all regions of the world, including tropical rainforest, arid desert, extremely cold arctic regions, and heavily polluted cities; in comparison, most other species are confined to a few geographical areas by their limited adaptability.[123] The human population is not, however, uniformly distributed on the Earth's surface, because the population density varies from one region to another, and large stretches of surface are almost completely uninhabited, like Antarctica and vast swathes of the ocean.[122][124] Most humans (61%) live in Asia; the remainder live in the Americas (14%), Africa (14%), Europe (11%), and Oceania

(0.5%).[125]

Within the last century, humans have explored challenging environments such as Antarctica, the deep sea, and outer space.[126] Human habitation within these hostile environments is restrictive and expensive, typically limited in duration, and restricted to scientific, military, or industrial expeditions.[126] Humans have briefly visited the Moon and made their presence felt on other celestial bodies through human-made robotic spacecraft.[127][128][129] Since the early 20th century, there has been continuous human presence in Antarctica through research stations and, since 2000, in space through habitation on the International Space Station.[130]

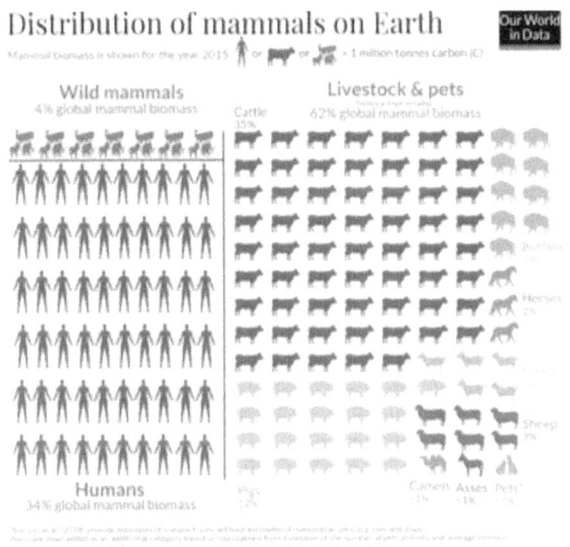

Enter Caption

Estimates of the population at the time agriculture emerged in around 10,000 BC and have ranged between 1 million and 15 million.[132][133] Around 50–60 million people lived in the combined eastern and western Roman Empire in the 4th century AD.[134] Bubonic plagues, first recorded in the 6th century AD, reduced the population by 50%, with the Black Death killing 75–200 million people in Eurasia and North Africa alone.[135] Human population was believed to have reached one billion in 1800. It has since then increased exponentially, reaching two billion in 1930 and three billion in 1960, four in 1975, five in 1987 and six billion in 1999.[136] It passed seven billion in 2011 and 7.9 billion as of November 2021.[137] It took over two million years of human prehistory and history for the human population to reach one billion and only 207 years more to grow to 7 billion.[138] The combined biomass of the carbon of all the humans on Earth in 2018 was estimated at 60 million tons, about 10 times larger than that of all non-domesticated mammals.[131]

In 2018, 4.2 billion humans (55%) lived in urban areas, up from 751 million in 1950.[139] The most urbanized regions are Northern America (82%), Latin America (81%), Europe (74%) and Oceania (68%), with Africa and Asia having nearly 90% of the world's 3.4 billion rural population.[139] Problems for humans living in cities include various forms of pollution and crime,[140] especially in inner city and suburban slums. Humans have had a dramatic effect on the environment. They are apex predators, being rarely preyed upon by other species.[141] Human population growth, industrialization, land development, overconsumption and combustion of fossil fuels have led to environmental destruction and pollution that significantly contributes to the ongoing mass extinction of other forms of life.[142][143] They are the main contributor to global climate change,[144] which may accelerate the Holocene extinction.

CHAPTER THREE

Biology

Anatomy and Physiology

Most aspects of human physiology are closely homologous to corresponding aspects of animal physiology. The human body consists of the legs, the torso, the arms, the neck, and the head. An adult human body consists of about 100 trillion (1014) cells. The most commonly defined body systems in humans are the nervous, the cardiovascular, the digestive, the endocrine, the immune, the integumentary, the lymphatic, the musculoskeletal, the reproductive, the respiratory, and the urinary system.[146][147] The dental formula of humans is: 2.1.2.32.1.2.3. Humans have proportionately shorter palates and much smaller teeth than other primates. They are the only primates to have short, relatively flush canine teeth. Humans have characteristically crowded teeth, with gaps from lost teeth usually closing up quickly in young individuals. Humans are gradually losing their third molars, with some individuals having them congenitally absent.[148]

Humans share with chimpanzees a vestigial tail, appendix, flexible shoulder joints, grasping fingers and opposable thumbs.[149] Apart from bipedalism and brain size, humans differ from chimpanzees mostly in smelling, hearing and digesting proteins.[150] While humans have a density of hair follicles comparable to other apes, it is predominately vellus hair, most of which is so short and wispy as to be practically invisible.[151][152] Humans have about 2 million sweat glands spread over their entire bodies, many more than chimpanzees, whose sweat glands are scarce and are mainly located on the palm of the hand and on the soles of the feet.[153]

It is estimated that the worldwide average height for an adult human male is about 171 cm (5 ft 7 in), while the worldwide average height for adult human females is about 159 cm (5 ft 3 in).[154] Shrinkage of stature may begin in middle age in some individuals but tends to be typical in the extremely aged.[155] Throughout history, human populations have universally become taller, probably as a consequence of better nutrition, healthcare, and living conditions.[156] The average mass of an adult human is 59 kg (130 lb) for females and 77 kg (170 lb) for males.[157][158] Like many other conditions, body weight and body type are influenced by both genetic susceptibility and environment and varies greatly among individuals.[159][160]

Humans have a far faster and more accurate throw than other animals.[161] Humans are also among the best long-distance runners in the animal kingdom, but slower over short distances.[162][150] Humans' thinner body hair and more productive sweat glands help avoid heat exhaustion while running for long distances.

Genetics

Like most animals, humans are a diploid and eukaryotic species. Each somatic cell has two sets of 23 chromosomes, each set received from one parent; gametes have only one set of chromosomes, which is a mixture of the two parental sets. Among the 23 pairs of chromosomes, there are 22 pairs of autosomes and one pair of sex chromosomes. Like other mammals, humans have an XY sex-determination system, so that females have the sex chromosomes XX and males have XY.[164] Genes and environment influence human biological variation in visible characteristics, physiology, disease susceptibility and mental abilities. The exact influence of genes and environment on certain traits is not well understood.[165][166]

While no humans—not even monozygotic twins—are genetically identical,[167] two humans on average will have a genetic similarity of 99.5%-99.9%.[168][169] This makes them more homogeneous than other great apes, including chimpanzees.[170][171] This small variation in human DNA compared to many other species suggests a population bottleneck during the Late Pleistocene (around 100,000 years ago), in which the human population was reduced to a small number of breeding pairs.[172][173] The forces of natural selection have continued to operate on human populations, with evidence that certain regions of the genome display directional selection in the past 15,000 years.[174]

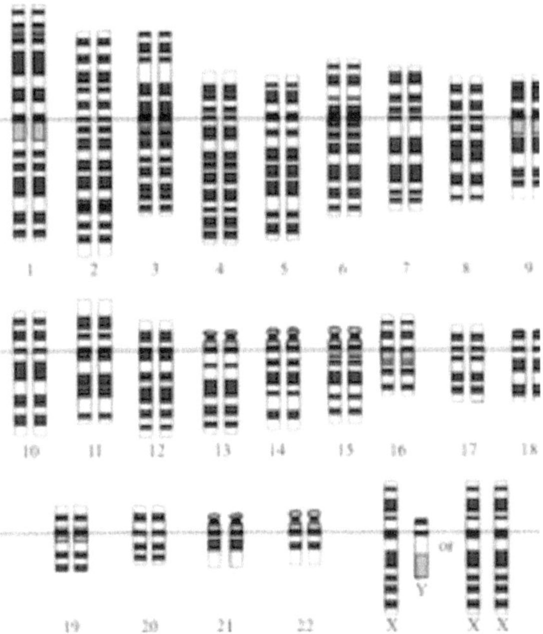

A graphical representation of the standard human karyotype, including both the male (XY) and female (XX) sex chromosomes.

Enter Caption

The human genome was first sequenced in 2001[175] and by 2020 hundreds of thousands of genomes had been sequenced.[176] In 2012 the International HapMap Project had compared the genomes of 1,184 individuals from 11 populations and identified 1.6 million single nucleotide polymorphisms.[177] African populations harbor the highest number of private genetic variants. While many of the common variants found in populations outside of Africa are also found on the African continent, there are still large numbers that are private to these regions, especially Oceania and the Americas.[178] By 2010 estimates, humans have approximately 22,000 genes.[179] By comparing mitochondrial DNA, which is inherited only from the mother, geneticists have concluded that the last female common ancestor whose genetic marker is found in all modern humans, the so-called mitochondrial Eve, must have lived around 90,000 to 200,000 years ago.

Life Cycle

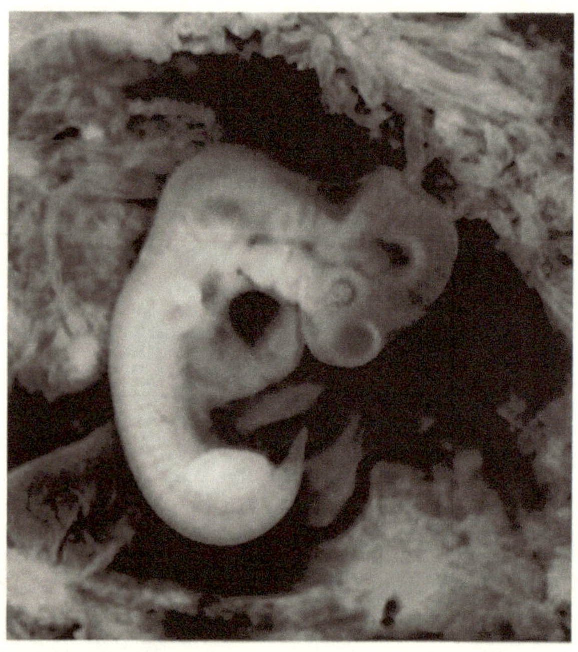

A 10 mm human embryo at 5 weeks

Enter Caption

Most human reproduction takes place by internal fertilization via sexual intercourse, but can also occur through assisted reproductive technology procedures.[184] The average gestation period is 38 weeks, but a normal pregnancy can vary by up to 37 days.[185] Embryonic development in the human covers the first eight weeks of development; at the beginning of the ninth week the embryo is termed a fetus.[186] Humans are able to induce early labor or perform a caesarean section if the child needs to be born earlier for medical reasons.[187] In developed countries, infants are typically 3–4 kg (7–9 lb) in weight and 47–53 cm (19–21 in) in height at birth.[188][189] However, low birth weight is common in developing countries, and contributes to the high levels of infant mortality in these regions.[190]

Compared with other species, human childbirth is dangerous, with a much higher risk of complications and death.[191] The size of the fetus's head is more closely matched to the pelvis than other primates.[192] The reason for this is not completely understood,[n 3] but it contributes to a painful labor that can last 24 hours or more.[194] The chances of a successful labor increased significantly during the 20th century in wealthier countries with the advent of new medical technologies. In contrast, pregnancy and natural childbirth remain hazardous ordeals in developing regions of the world, with maternal death rates approximately 100 times greater than in developed countries.[195]

Both the mother and the father provide care for human offspring, in contrast to other primates, where parental care is mostly done by the mother.[196] Helpless at birth, humans continue to grow for some years, typically reaching sexual maturity at 15 to 17 years of age.[197][198][199] The human life span has been split into various stages ranging from three to twelve. Common stages include infancy, childhood, adolescence, adulthood and old age.[200] The lengths of these stages have varied across cultures and time periods but is typified by an unusually rapid growth spurt during adolescence.[201] Human females undergo menopause and become infertile at around the age of 50.[202] It has been proposed that menopause increases a woman's overall reproductive success by allowing her to invest more time and resources in her existing offspring, and in turn their children (the grandmother hypothesis), rather than by continuing to bear children into old age.[203][204]

The life span of an individual depends on two major factors, genetics and lifestyle choices.[205] For various reasons, including biological/genetic causes, women live on average about four years longer than men.[206] As of 2018, the global average life expectancy at birth of a girl is estimated to be 74.9 years compared to 70.4 for a boy.[207][208] There are significant geographical variations in human life expectancy, mostly correlated with economic development—for example, life expectancy at birth in Hong Kong is 87.6 years for girls and 81.8 for boys, while in the Central African Republic, it is 55.0 years for girls and 50.6 for boys.[209][210] The developed world is generally aging, with the median age around 40 years. In the developing world, the median age is between 15 and 20 years. While one in five Europeans is 60 years of age or older, only one in twenty Africans is 60 years of age or older.[211] The number of centenarians (humans of age 100 years or older) in the world was estimated by the

United Nations at 210,000 in 2002.

Diet

Humans are omnivorous, capable of consuming a wide variety of plant and animal material.[213][214] Human groups have adopted a range of diets from purely vegan to primarily carnivorous. In some cases, dietary restrictions in humans can lead to deficiency diseases; however, stable human groups have adapted to many dietary patterns through both genetic specialization and cultural conventions to use nutritionally balanced food sources.[215] The human diet is prominently reflected in human culture and has led to the development of food science.[216]

Until the development of agriculture approximately 10,000 years ago, Homo sapiens employed a hunter-gatherer method as their sole means of food collection.[216] This involved combining stationary food sources (such as fruits, grains, tubers, and mushrooms, insect larvae and aquatic mollusks) with wild game, which must be hunted and captured in order to be consumed.[217] It has been proposed that humans have used fire to prepare and cook food since the time of Homo erectus.[218] Around ten thousand years ago, humans developed agriculture,[219][220][221] which substantially altered their diet. This change in diet may also have altered human biology; with the spread of dairy farming providing a new and rich source of food, leading to the evolution of the ability to digest lactose in some adults.[222][223] The types of food consumed, and how they are prepared, have varied widely by time, location, and culture.[224][225]

In general, humans can survive for up to eight weeks without food, depending on stored body fat.[226] Survival without water is usually limited to three or four days, with a maximum of one week.[227] In 2020 it is estimated 9 million humans die every year from causes directly or indirectly related to starvation.[228][229] Childhood malnutrition is also common and contributes to the global burden of disease.[230] However, global food distribution is not even, and obesity among some human populations has increased rapidly, leading to health complications and increased mortality in some developed and a few developing countries. Worldwide, over one billion people are obese,[231] while in the United States 35% of people are obese, leading to this being described as an "obesity epidemic."[232] Obesity is caused by consuming more calories than are expended, so excessive weight gain is usually caused by an energy-dense diet.

Biological Variation

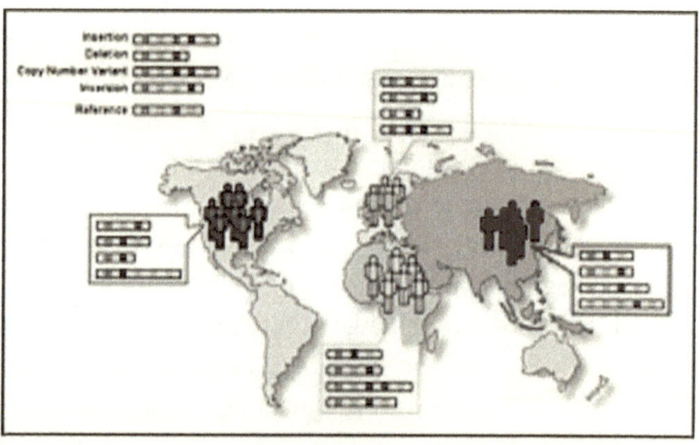

Changes in the number and order of genes (A-D) create genetic diversity within and between population

Enter Caption

There is biological variation in the human species—with traits such as blood type, genetic diseases, cranial features, facial features, organ systems, eye color, hair color and texture, height and build, and skin color varying across the globe. The typical height of an adult human is between 1.4 and 1.9 m (4 ft 7 in and 6 ft 3 in), although this varies significantly depending on sex, ethnic origin, and family bloodlines.[233][234] Body size is partly determined by genes and is also significantly influenced by environmental factors such as diet, exercise, and sleep patterns.[235]

There is evidence that populations have adapted genetically to various external factors. The genes that allow adult humans to digest lactose are present in high frequencies in populations that have long histories of cattle domestication and are more dependent on cow milk.[236] Sickle cell anemia, which may provide increased resistance to malaria, is frequent in populations where malaria is endemic.[237][238] Populations that have for a very long time inhabited specific climates tend to have developed specific phenotypes that are beneficial for those environments—short stature and stocky build in cold regions, tall and lanky in hot regions, and with high lung capacities or other adaptations at high altitudes.[239][240] Some populations have evolved highly unique adaptations to very specific environmental conditions, such as those advantageous to ocean-dwelling lifestyles and freediving in the Bajau.[241]

Human hair ranges in color from red to blond to brown to black, which is the most frequent.[242] Hair color depends on the amount of melanin, with concentrations fading with increased age, leading to grey or even white hair. Skin color can range from darkest brown to lightest peach, or even nearly white or colorless in cases of albinism.[243] It tends to vary clinally and generally correlates with the level of ultraviolet radiation in a particular geographic area, with darker skin mostly around the equator.[244] Skin darkening may have evolved as protection against ultraviolet solar radiation.[245] Light skin pigmentation protects against depletion of vitamin D, which requires sunlight to make.[246] Human skin also has a capacity to darken (tan) in response to exposure to ultraviolet radiation.

A Libyan, a Nubian, a Syrian, and an
Egyptian, drawing by an unknown
artist after a mural of the tomb of Seti
I.

Enter Caption

There is relatively little variation between human geographical populations, and most of the variation that occurs is at the individual level.[243][249][250] Much of human variation is continuous, often with no clear points of demarcation.[251][252][253][254] Genetic data shows that no matter how population groups are defined, two people from the same population group are almost as different from each other as two people from any two different population groups.[255][256][257] Dark-skinned populations that are found in Africa, Australia, and South Asia are not closely related to each other.[258][259]

Genetic research has demonstrated that human populations native to the African continent are the most genetically diverse[260] and genetic diversity decreases with migratory distance from Africa, possibly the result of bottlenecks during human migration.[261][262] These non-African populations acquired new genetic inputs from local admixture with archaic populations and have much greater variation from Neanderthals and Denisovans than is found in Africa,[178] though Neanderthal admixture into African populations may be underestimated.[263] Furthermore, recent studies have found that populations in sub-Saharan Africa, and particularly West Africa, have ancestral genetic variation which predates modern humans and has been lost in most non-African populations. Some of this ancestry is thought to originate from admixture with an unknown archaic hominin that diverged before the split of Neanderthals and modern humans.[264][265]

Humans are a gonochoric species, meaning they are divided into male and female sexes.[266][267][268] The greatest degree of genetic variation exists between males and females. While the nucleotide genetic variation of individuals of the same sex across global populations is no greater than 0.1%–0.5%, the genetic difference between males and females is between 1% and 2%. Males on average are 15% heavier and 15 cm (6 in) taller than females.[269][270] On average, men have about 40–50% more upper body strength and 20–30% more lower body strength than women at the same weight, due to higher amounts of muscle and larger muscle fibers.[271] Women generally have a higher body fat percentage than men.[272] Women have lighter skin than men of the same population; this has been explained by a higher need for vitamin D in females during pregnancy and lactation.[273] As there are chromosomal differences between females and males, some X and Y chromosome-related conditions and disorders only affect either men or women.[274] After allowing for body weight and volume, the male voice is usually an octave deeper than the female voice.[275] Women have a longer life span in almost every population around the world.

CHAPTER FOUR

Psychology

The Human Brain

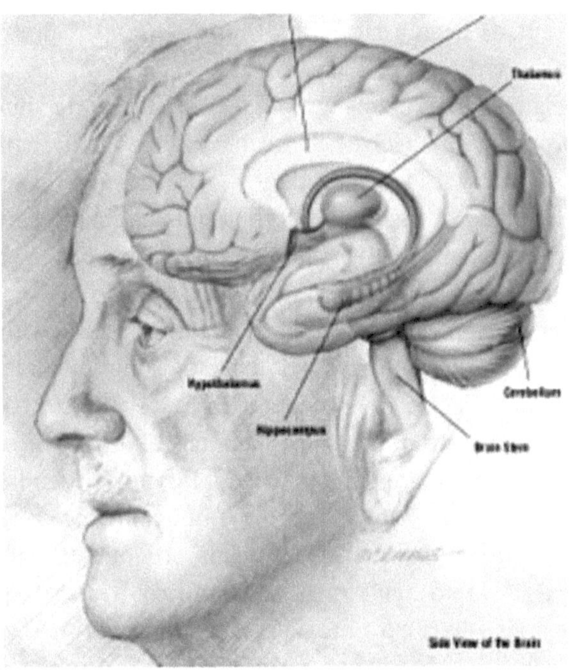

Drawing of the human brain, showing several important structures

Enter Caption

The human brain, the focal point of the central nervous system in humans, controls the peripheral nervous system. In addition to controlling "lower," involuntary, or primarily autonomic activities such as respiration and digestion, it is also the locus of "higher" order functioning such as thought, reasoning, and abstraction.[277] These cognitive processes constitute the mind, and, along with their behavioral consequences, are studied in the field of psychology.

Humans have a larger and more developed prefrontal cortex than other primates, the region of the brain associated with higher cognition.[278] This has led humans to proclaim themselves to be more intelligent than any other known species.[279] Objectively defining intelligence is difficult, with other animals adapting senses and excelling in areas that humans are unable to.[280]

There are some traits that, although not strictly unique, do set humans apart from other animals.[281] Humans may be the only animals who have episodic memory and who can engage in "mental time travel".[282] Even compared with other social animals, humans have an unusually high degree of flexibility in their facial expressions.[283] Humans are the only animals known to cry emotional tears.[284] Humans are one of the few animals able to self-recognize in mirror tests[285] and there is also debate over to what extent humans are the only animals with a theory of mind.

Sleep and Dreaming

Humans are generally diurnal. The average sleep requirement is between seven and nine hours per day for an adult and nine to ten hours per day for a child; elderly people usually sleep for six to seven hours. Having less sleep than this is common among humans, even though sleep deprivation can have negative health effects. A sustained restriction of adult sleep to four hours per day has been shown to correlate with changes in physiology and mental state, including reduced memory, fatigue, aggression, and bodily discomfort.[287]

During sleep humans dream, where they experience sensory images and sounds. Dreaming is stimulated by the pons and mostly occurs during the REM phase of sleep.[288] The length of a dream can vary, from a few seconds up to 30 minutes.[289] Humans have three to five dreams per night, and some may have up to seven;[290] however most dreams are immediately or quickly forgotten.[291] They are more likely to remember the dream if awakened during the REM phase. The events in dreams are generally outside the control of the dreamer, with the exception of lucid dreaming, where the dreamer is self-aware.[292] Dreams can at times make a creative thought occur or give a sense of inspiration.

Consciousness and Thought

Human consciousness, at its simplest, is "sentience or awareness of internal or external existence".[294] Despite centuries of analyses, definitions, explanations and debates by philosophers and scientists, consciousness remains puzzling and controversial,[295] being "at once the most familiar and most mysterious aspect of our lives".[296] The only widely agreed notion about the topic is the intuition that it exists.[297] Opinions differ about what exactly needs to be studied and explained as consciousness. Some philosophers divide consciousness into phenomenal consciousness, which is sensory experience itself, and access consciousness, which can be used for reasoning or directly controlling actions.[298] It is sometimes synonymous with 'the mind', and at other times, an aspect of it. Historically it is associated with introspection, private thought, imagination and volition.[299] It now often includes some kind of experience, cognition, feeling or perception. It may be 'awareness', or 'awareness of awareness', or self-awareness.[300] There might be different levels or orders of consciousness,[301] or different kinds of consciousness, or just one kind with different features.[302]

The process of acquiring knowledge and understanding through thought, experience, and the senses is known as cognition.[303] The human brain perceives the external world through the senses, and each individual human is influenced greatly by his or her experiences, leading to subjective views of existence and the passage of time.[304] The nature of thought is central to psychology and related fields. Cognitive psychology studies cognition, the mental processes underlying behavior.[305] Largely focusing on the development of the human mind through the life span, developmental psychology seeks to understand how people come to perceive, understand, and act within the world and how these processes change as they age.[306][307] This may focus on intellectual, cognitive, neural, social, or moral development. Psychologists have developed intelligence tests and the concept of intelligence quotient in order to assess the relative intelligence of human beings and study its distribution among population.

Motivation and emotion

Illustration of grief from Charles Darwin's 1872 book *The Expression of the Emotions in Man and Animals.*

Enter Caption

Human motivation is not yet wholly understood. From a psychological perspective, Maslow's hierarchy of needs is a well-established theory that can be defined as the process of satisfying certain needs in ascending order of complexity.[309] From a more general, philosophical perspective, human motivation can be defined as a commitment to, or withdrawal from, various goals requiring the application of human ability. Furthermore, incentive and preference are both factors, as are any perceived links between incentives and preferences. Volition may also be involved, in which case willpower is also a factor. Ideally, both motivation and volition ensure the selection, striving for, and realization of goals in an optimal manner, a function beginning in childhood and continuing throughout a lifetime in a process known as socialization.[310]

Emotions are biological states associated with the nervous system[311][312] brought on by neurophysiological changes variously associated with thoughts, feelings, behavioral responses, and a degree of pleasure or displeasure.[313][314] They are often intertwined with mood, temperament, personality, disposition, creativity,[315] and motivation. Emotion has a significant influence on human behavior and their ability to learn.[316] Acting on extreme or uncontrolled emotions can lead to social disorder and crime,[317] with studies showing criminals may have a lower emotional intelligence than normal.[318]

Emotional experiences perceived as pleasant, such as joy, interest or contentment, contrast with those perceived as unpleasant, like anxiety, sadness, anger, and despair.[319] Happiness, or the state of being happy, is a human emotional condition. The definition of happiness is a common philosophical topic. Some define it as experiencing the feeling of positive emotional affects, while avoiding the negative ones.[320][321] Others see it as an appraisal of life satisfaction or quality of life.[322] Recent research suggests that being happy might involve experiencing some negative emotions when humans feel they are warranted.

Sexuality and Love

Parents can display familial love for their children

Enter Caption

For humans, sexuality involves biological, erotic, physical, emotional, social, or spiritual feelings and behaviors.[324][325] Because it is a broad term, which has varied with historical contexts over time, it lacks a precise definition.[325] The biological and physical aspects of sexuality largely concern the human reproductive functions, including the human sexual response cycle.[324][325] Sexuality also affects and is affected by cultural, political, legal, philosophical, moral, ethical, and religious aspects of life.[324][325] Sexual desire, or libido, is a basic mental state present at the beginning of sexual behavior. Studies show that men desire sex more than women and masturbate more often.[326]

Humans can fall anywhere along a continuous scale of sexual orientation,[327] although most humans are heterosexual.[328][329] While homosexual behavior occurs in some other animals, only humans and domestic sheep have so far been found to exhibit exclusive preference for same-sex relationships.[328] Most evidence supports nonsocial, biological causes of sexual orientation,[328] as cultures that are very tolerant of homosexuality do not have significantly higher rates of it.[329][330] Research in neuroscience and genetics suggests that other aspects of human sexuality are biologically influenced as well.[331]

Love most commonly refers to a feeling of strong attraction or emotional attachment. It can be impersonal (the love of an object, ideal, or strong political or spiritual connection) or interpersonal (love between humans).[332] When in love dopamine, norepinephrine, serotonin and other chemicals stimulate the brain's pleasure center, leading to side effects such as increased heart rate, loss of appetite and sleep, and an intense feeling of excitement.

CHAPTER FIVE

Culture and Society

Culture

Humanity's unprecedented set of intellectual skills were a key factor in the species' eventual technological advancement and concomitant domination of the biosphere.[337] Disregarding extinct hominids, humans are the only animals known to teach generalizable information,[338] innately deploy recursive embedding to generate and communicate complex concepts,[339] engage in the "folk physics" required for competent tool design,[340][341] or cook food in the wild.[342] Teaching and learning preserves the cultural and ethnographic identity of human societies.[343] Other traits and behaviors that are mostly unique to humans include starting fires,[344] phoneme structuring[345] and vocal learning.

Language

While many species communicate, language is unique to humans, a defining feature of humanity, and a cultural universal.[347] Unlike the limited systems of other animals, human language is open—an infinite number of meanings can be produced by combining a limited number of symbols.[348][349] Human language also has the capacity of displacement, using words to represent things and happenings that are not presently or locally occurring but reside in the shared imagination of interlocutors.[148]

Language differs from other forms of communication in that it is modality independent; the same meanings can be conveyed through different media, audibly in speech, visually by sign language or writing, and through tactile media such as braille.[350] Language is central to the communication between humans, and to the sense of identity that unites nations, cultures and ethnic groups.[351] There are approximately six thousand different languages currently in use, including sign languages, and many thousands more that are extinct.

The Arts

Human arts can take many forms including visual, literary and performing. Visual art can range from paintings and sculptures to film, interaction design and architecture.[353] Literary arts can include prose, poetry and dramas; while the performing arts generally involve theatre, music and dance.[354][355] Humans often combine the different forms (for example, music videos).[356] Other entities that have been described as having artistic qualities include food preparation, video games and medicine.[357][358][359] As well as providing entertainment and transferring knowledge, the arts are also used for political purposes.

Art is a defining characteristic of humans and there is evidence for a relationship between creativity and language.[361] The earliest evidence of art was shell engravings made by Homo erectus 300,000 years before modern humans evolved.[362] Art attributed to H. sapiens existed at least 75,000 years ago, with jewellery and drawings found in caves in South Africa.[363][364] There are various hypotheses as to why humans have adapted to the arts. These include allowing them to better problem solve issues, providing a means to control or influence other humans, encouraging cooperation and contribution within a society or increasing the chance of attracting a potential mate.[365] The use of imagination developed through art, combined with logic may have given early humans an evolutionary advantage.[361]

Evidence of humans engaging in musical activities predates cave art and so far music has been practiced by virtually all known human cultures.[366] There exists a wide variety of music genres and ethnic musics; with humans' musical abilities being related to other abilities, including complex social human behaviours.[366] It has been shown that human brains respond to music by becoming synchronized with the rhythm and beat, a process called entrainment.[367] Dance is also a form of human expression found in all cultures[368] and may have evolved as a way to help early humans communicate.[369] Listening to music and observing dance stimulates the orbitofrontal cortex and other pleasure sensing areas of the brain.[370]

Unlike speaking, reading and writing does not come naturally to humans and must be taught.[371] Still, literature has been present before the invention of words and language, with 30,000-year-old paintings on walls inside some caves portraying a series of dramatic scenes.[372] One of the oldest surviving works of literature is the Epic of Gilgamesh, first engraved on ancient Babylonian tablets about 4,000 years ago.[373] Beyond simply passing down knowledge, the use and sharing of imaginative fiction through stories might have helped develop humans' capabilities for communication and increased the likelihood of securing a mate.[374]

Storytelling may also be used as a way to provide the audience with moral lessons and encourage cooperation.

Tools and Technologies

Stone tools were used by proto-humans at least 2.5 million years ago.[376] The use and manufacture of tools has been put forward as the ability that defines humans more than anything else[377] and has historically been seen as an important evolutionary step.[378] The technology became much more sophisticated about 1.8 million years ago,[377] with the controlled use of fire beginning around 1 million years ago.[379][380] The wheel and wheeled vehicles appeared simultaneously in several regions some time in the fourth millennium BC.[60] The development of more complex tools and technologies allowed land to be cultivated and animals to be domesticated, thus proving essential in the development of agriculture—what is known as the Neolithic Revolution.[381]

China developed paper, the printing press, gunpowder, the compass and other important inventions.[382] The continued improvements in smelting allowed forging of copper, bronze, iron and eventually steel, which is used in railways, skyscrapers and many other products.[383] This coincided with the Industrial Revolution, where the invention of automated machines brought major changes to humans' lifestyles.[384] Modern technology is observed as progressing exponentially,[385] with major innovations in the 20th century including: electricity, penicillin, semiconductors, internal combustion engines, the Internet, nitrogen fixing fertilisers, airplanes, computers, automobiles, contraceptive pills, nuclear fission, the green revolution, radio, scientific plant breeding, rockets, air conditioning, television and the assembly line.

Religion and Spirituality

Religion is generally defined as a belief system concerning the supernatural, sacred or divine, and practices, values, institutions and rituals associated with such belief. Some religions also have a moral code. The evolution and the history of the first religions have recently become areas of active scientific investigation.[387][388][389][390] While the exact time when humans first became religious remains unknown, research shows credible evidence of religious behaviour from around the Middle Paleolithic era (45-200 thousand years ago).[391] It may have evolved to play a role in helping enforce and encourage cooperation between humans.[392]

There is no accepted academic definition of what constitutes religion.[393] Religion has taken on many forms that vary by culture and individual perspective in alignment with the geographic, social, and linguistic diversity of the planet.[393] Religion can include a belief in life after death (commonly involving belief in an afterlife),[394] the origin of life,[395] the nature of the universe (religious cosmology) and its ultimate fate (eschatology), and what is moral or immoral.[396] A common source for answers to these questions are beliefs in transcendent divine beings such as deities or a singular God, although not all religions are theistic.[397][398]

Although the exact level of religiosity can be hard to measure,[399] a majority of humans profess some variety of religious or spiritual belief.[400] In 2015 the plurality were Christian followed by Muslims, Hindus and Buddhists.[401] As of 2015, about 16%, or slightly under 1.2 billion humans, were irreligious, including those with no religious beliefs or no identity with any religion.

Science and Philosophy

An aspect unique to humans is their ability to transmit knowledge from one generation to the next and to continually build on this information to develop tools, scientific laws and other advances to pass on further.[403] This accumulated knowledge can be tested to answer questions or make predictions about how the universe functions and has been very successful in advancing human ascendancy.[404] Aristotle has been described as the first scientist,[405] and preceded the rise of scientific thought through the Hellenistic period.[406] Other early advances in science came from the Han Dynasty in China and during the Islamic Golden Age.[407][85] The scientific revolution, near the end of the Renaissance, led to the emergence of modern science.[408]

A chain of events and influences led to the development of the scientific method, a process of observation and experimentation that is used to differentiate science from pseudoscience.[409] An understanding of mathematics is unique to humans, although other species of animals have some numerical cognition.[410] All of science can be divided into three major branches, the formal sciences (e.g., logic and mathematics), which are concerned with formal systems, the applied sciences (e.g., engineering, medicine), which are focused on practical applications, and the empirical sciences, which are based on empirical observation and are in turn divided into natural sciences (e.g., physics, chemistry, biology) and social sciences (e.g., psychology, economics, sociology).[411]

Philosophy is a field of study where humans seek to understand fundamental truths about themselves and the world in which they live.[412] Philosophical inquiry has been a major feature in the development of humans' intellectual history.[413] It has been described as the "no man's land" between definitive scientific knowledge and dogmatic religious teachings.[414] Philosophy relies on reason and evidence, unlike religion, but does not require the empirical observations and experiments provided by science.[415] Major fields of philosophy include metaphysics, epistemology, logic, and axiology (which includes ethics and aesthetics).

Society

Society is the system of organizations and institutions arising from interaction between humans. Humans are highly social and tend to live in large complex social groups. They can be divided into different groups according to their income, wealth, power, reputation and other factors. The structure of social stratification and the degree of social mobility differs, especially between modern and traditional societies.[417][unreliable source?] Human groups range from the size of families to nations. The first form of human social organization is thought to have resembled hunter-gatherer band societies.

Gender

Human societies typically exhibit gender identities and gender roles that distinguish between masculine and feminine characteristics and prescribe the range of acceptable behaviours and attitudes for their members based on their sex.[419][420] The most common categorisation is a gender binary of men and women.[421] Many societies recognise a third gender,[422] or less commonly a fourth or fifth.[423][424] In some other societies, non-binary is used as an umbrella term for a range of gender identities that are not solely male or female.[425]

Gender roles are often associated with a division of norms, practices, dress, behavior, rights, duties, privileges, status, and power.[citation needed] As a social construct,[426] gender roles are not fixed and vary historically within a society. Challenges to predominant gender norms have recurred in many societies.[427][428] Little is known about gender roles in the earliest human societies. Early modern humans probably had a range of gender roles similar to that of modern cultures from at least the Upper Paleolithic, while the Neanderthals were less sexually dimorphic and there is evidence that the behavioural difference between males and females was minimal.

Kinship

All human societies organize, recognize and classify types of social relationships based on relations between parents, children and other descendants (consanguinity), and relations through marriage (affinity). There is also a third type applied to godparents or adoptive children (fictive). These culturally defined relationships are referred to as kinship. In many societies, it is one of the most important social organizing principles and plays a role in transmitting status and inheritance.[430] All societies have rules of incest taboo, according to which marriage between certain kinds of kin relations are prohibited, and some also have rules of preferential marriage with certain kin relations.

Ethnicity

Human ethnic groups are a social category that identifies together as a group based on shared attributes that distinguish them from other groups. These can be a common set of traditions, ancestry, language, history, society, culture, nation, religion, or social treatment within their residing area.[432][433] Ethnicity is separate from the concept of race, which is based on physical characteristics, although both are socially constructed.[434] Assigning ethnicity to a certain population is complicated, as even within common ethnic designations there can be a diverse range of subgroups, and the makeup of these ethnic groups can change over time at both the collective and individual level.[170] Also, there is no generally accepted definition of what constitutes an ethnic group.[435] Ethnic groupings can play a powerful role in the social identity and solidarity of ethnopolitical units. This has been closely tied to the rise of the nation state as the predominant form of political organization in the 19th and 20th centuries.

Government and Politics

As farming populations gathered in larger and denser communities, interactions between these different groups increased. This led to the development of governance within and between the communities.[439] Humans have evolved the ability to change affiliation with various social groups relatively easily, including previously strong political alliances, if doing so is seen as providing personal advantages.[440] This cognitive flexibility allows individual humans to change their political ideologies, with those with higher flexibility less likely to support authoritarian and nationalistic stances.[441]

Governments create laws and policies that affect the citizens that they govern. There have been many forms of government throughout human history, each having various means of obtaining power and the ability to exert diverse controls on the population.[442] As of 2017, more than half of all national governments are democracies, with 13% being autocracies and 28% containing elements of both.[443] Many countries have formed international political organizations and alliances, the largest being the United Nations with 193 member states.

Trade and Economics

Trade, the voluntary exchange of goods and services, is seen as a characteristic that differentiates humans from other animals and has been cited as a practice that gave Homo sapiens a major advantage over other hominids.[445] Evidence suggests early H. sapiens made use of long-distance trade routes to exchange goods and ideas, leading to cultural explosions and providing additional food sources when hunting was sparse, while such trade networks did not exist for the now extinct Neanderthals.[446][447] Early trade likely involved materials for creating tools like obsidian.[448] The first truly international trade routes were around the spice trade through the Roman and medieval periods.[449]

Early human economies were more likely to be based around gift giving instead of a bartering system.[450] Early money consisted of commodities; the oldest being in the form of cattle and the most widely used being cowrie shells.[451] Money has since evolved into governmental issued coins, paper and electronic money.[451] Human study of economics is a social science that looks at how societies distribute scarce resources among different people.[452] There are massive inequalities in the division of wealth among humans; the eight richest humans are worth the same monetary value as the poorest half of all the human population.

Conflict

Humans commit violence on other humans at a rate comparable to other primates, but kill adult humans at a high rate (with infanticide being more common among other primates).[454] It is predicted that 2% of early H. sapiens would be murdered, rising to 12% during the medieval period, before dropping to below 2% in modern times.[455] There is great variation in violence between human populations with rates of homicide in societies that have legal systems and strong cultural attitudes against violence at about 0.01%.[456]

The willingness of humans to kill other members of their species en masse through organized conflict (i.e., war) has long been the subject of debate. One school of thought is that war evolved as a means to eliminate competitors, and has always been an innate human characteristic. Another suggests that war is a relatively recent phenomenon and appeared due to changing social conditions.[457] While not settled, the current evidence suggests warlike predispositions only became common about 10,000 years ago, and in many places much more recently than that.[457] War has had a high cost on human life; it is estimated that during the 20th century, between 167 million and 188 million people died as a result of war.

CHAPTER SIX

The Sun

The Sun is the star at the center of the Solar System. It is a nearly perfect ball of hot plasma,[18][19] heated to incandescence by nuclear fusion reactions in its core, radiating the energy mainly as light, ultraviolet, and infrared radiation. It is the most important source of energy for life on Earth.

The Sun's diameter is about 1.39 million kilometers (864,000 miles), or 109 times that of Earth. Its mass is about 330,000 times that of Earth, comprising about 99.86% of the total mass of the Solar System.[20] Roughly three-quarters of the Sun's mass consists of hydrogen (~73%); the rest is mostly helium (~25%), with much smaller quantities of heavier elements, including oxygen, carbon, neon, and iron.[21]

The Sun is a G-type main-sequence star (G2V). As such, it is informally, and not completely accurately, referred to as a yellow dwarf (its light is actually white). It formed approximately 4.6 billion[a][14][22] years ago from the gravitational collapse of matter within a region of a large molecular cloud. Most of this matter gathered in the center, whereas the rest flattened into an orbiting disk that became the Solar System. The central mass became so hot and dense that it eventually initiated nuclear fusion in its core.

It is thought that almost all stars form by this process.

Every second, the Sun's core fuses about 600 million tons of hydrogen into helium, and in the process converts 4 million tons of matter into energy. This energy, which can take between 10,000 and 170,000 years to escape the core, is the source of the Sun's light and heat. When hydrogen fusion in its core has diminished to the point at which the Sun is no longer in hydrostatic equilibrium, its core will undergo a marked increase in density and temperature while its outer layers expand, eventually transforming the Sun into a red giant. It is calculated that the Sun will become sufficiently large to engulf the current orbits of Mercury and Venus, and render Earth uninhabitable – but not for about five billion years. After this, it will shed its outer layers and become a dense type of cooling star known as a white dwarf, and no longer produce energy by fusion, but still glow and give off heat from its previous fusion.

The enormous effect of the Sun on Earth has been recognized since prehistoric times. The Sun was thought of by some cultures as a deity. The synodic rotation of Earth and its orbit around the Sun are the basis of some solar calendars. The predominant calendar in use today is the Gregorian calendar which is based upon the standard 16th-century interpretation of the Sun's observed movement as actual movement.

Etimology

The English word sun developed from Old English sunne. Cognates appear in other Germanic languages, including West Frisian sinne, Dutch zon, Low German Sünn, Standard German Sonne, Bavarian Sunna, Old Norse sunna, and Gothic sunnō. All these words stem from Proto-Germanic *sunnōn.[24][25] This is ultimately related to the word for sun in other branches of the Indo-European language family, though in most cases a nominative stem with an l is found, rather than the genitive stem in n, as for example in Latin sōl, ancient Greek ἥλιος (hēlios), Welsh haul and Russian солнце (solntse; pronounced sontse), as well as (with *l > r) Sanskrit स्वर (svár) and Persian خور (xvar). Indeed, the l-stem survived in Proto-Germanic as well, as *sōwelan, which gave rise to Gothic sauil (alongside sunnō) and Old Norse prosaic sól (alongside poetic sunna), and through it the words for sun in the modern Scandinavian languages: Swedish and Danish solen, Icelandic sólin, etc.[25]

The principal adjectives for the Sun in English are sunny for sunlight and, in technical contexts, solar (/ˈsoʊlər/),[3] from Latin sol[26] – the latter found in terms such as solar day, solar eclipse and Solar System (occasionally Sol system). From the Greek helios comes the rare adjective heliac (/ˈhiːliæk/).[27] In English, the Greek and Latin words occur in poetry as personifications of the Sun, Helios (/ˈhiːliəs/) and Sol (/ˈsɒl/),[2][1] while in science fiction Sol may be used as a name for the Sun to distinguish it from other stars. The term sol with a lower-case s is used by planetary astronomers for the duration of a solar day on another planet such as Mars.[28]

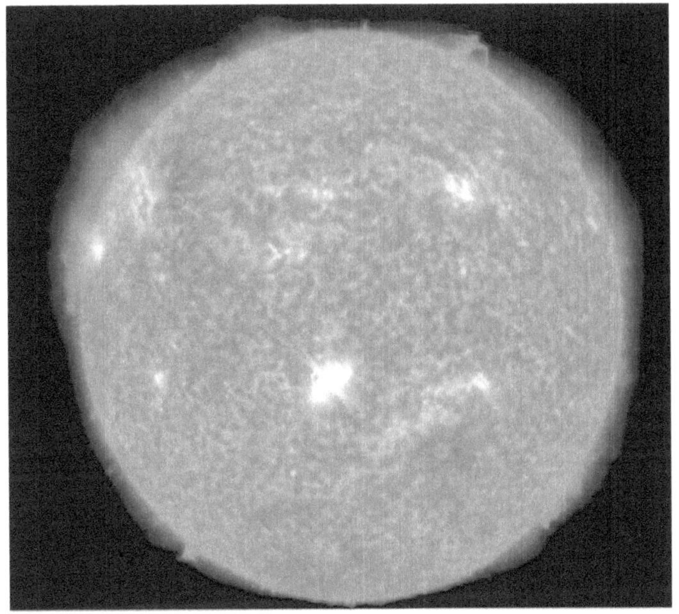

Enter Caption

The English weekday name Sunday stems from Old English Sunnandæg "sun's day", a Germanic interpretation of the Latin phrase diēs sōlis, itself a translation of the ancient Greek ἡμέρα ἡλίου (hēmera hēliou) 'day of the sun'.[29] The astronomical symbol for the Sun is a circle with a center dot, . It is used for such units as M⊙ (Solar mass), R⊙ (Solar radius) and L⊙ (Solar luminosity).

General Characteristics

The Sun is a G-type main-sequence star that constitutes about 99.86% of the mass of the Solar System. The Sun has an absolute magnitude of +4.83, estimated to be brighter than about 85% of the stars in the Milky Way, most of which are red dwarfs.[30][31] The Sun is a Population I, or heavy-element-rich,[b] star.[32] The formation of the Sun may have been triggered by shockwaves from one or more nearby supernovae.[33] This is suggested by a high abundance of heavy elements in the Solar System, such as gold and uranium, relative to the abundances of these elements in so-called Population II, heavy-element-poor, stars. The heavy elements could most plausibly have been produced by endothermic nuclear reactions during a supernova, or by transmutation through neutron absorption within a massive second-generation star.[32]

The Sun is by far the brightest object in the Earth's sky, with an apparent magnitude of −26.74.[34][35] This is about 13 billion times brighter than the next brightest star, Sirius, which has an apparent magnitude of −1.46. One astronomical unit (about 150,000,000 km; 93,000,000 mi) is defined as the mean distance of the Sun's center to Earth's center, though the distance varies as Earth moves from perihelion in January to aphelion in July.[36] The distances can vary between 147,098,074 km (perihelion) and 152,097,701 km (aphelion), and extreme values can range from 147,083,346 km to 152,112,126 km.[37] At its average distance, light travels from the Sun's horizon to Earth's horizon in about 8 minutes and 20 seconds,[38] while light from the closest points of the Sun and Earth takes about two seconds less. The energy of this sunlight supports almost all life[c] on Earth by photosynthesis,[39] and drives Earth's climate and weather.

The Sun does not have a definite boundary, but its density decreases exponentially with increasing height above the photosphere.[40] For the purpose of measurement, the Sun's radius is considered to be the distance from its center to the edge of the photosphere, the apparent visible surface of the Sun.[41] By this measure, the Sun is a near-perfect sphere with an oblateness estimated at 9 millionths,[42] which means that its polar diameter differs from its equatorial diameter by only 10 kilometers (6.2 mi).[43] The tidal effect of the planets is weak and does not significantly affect the shape of the Sun.[44] The Sun rotates faster at its equator than at its poles. This differential rotation is caused by convective motion due to heat transport and the Coriolis force due to the Sun's rotation. In a frame of reference defined by the stars, the rotational period is approximately 25.6 days at the equator and 33.5 days at the poles. Viewed from Earth as it orbits the Sun, the apparent rotational period of the Sun at its equator is about 28 days.[45] Viewed from a vantage point above its north pole, the Sun rotates counterclockwise around its axis of spin.

Composition

The Sun is composed primarily of the chemical elements hydrogen and helium. At this time in the Sun's life, they account for 74.9% and 23.8% of the mass of the Sun in the photosphere, respectively.[47] All heavier elements, called metals in astronomy, account for less than 2% of the mass, with oxygen (roughly 1% of the Sun's mass), carbon (0.3%), neon (0.2%), and iron (0.2%) being the most abundant.[48]

The Sun's original chemical composition was inherited from the interstellar medium out of which it formed. Originally it would have contained about 71.1% hydrogen, 27.4% helium, and 1.5% heavier elements.[47] The hydrogen and most of the helium in the Sun would have been produced by Big Bang nucleosynthesis in the first 20 minutes of the universe, and the heavier elements were produced by previous generations of stars before the Sun was formed, and spread into the interstellar medium during the final stages of stellar life and by events such as supernovae.[49]

Since the Sun formed, the main fusion process has involved fusing hydrogen into helium. Over the past 4.6 billion years, the amount of helium and its location within the Sun has gradually changed. Within the core, the proportion of helium has increased from about 24% to about 60% due to fusion, and some of the helium and heavy elements have settled from the photosphere towards the center of the Sun because of gravity. The proportions of heavier elements is unchanged. Heat is transferred outward from the Sun's core by radiation rather than by convection (see Radiative zone below), so the fusion products are not lifted outward by heat; they remain in the core[50] and gradually an inner core of helium has begun to form that cannot be fused because presently the Sun's core is not hot or dense enough to fuse helium. In the current photosphere, the helium fraction is reduced, and the metallicity is only 84% of what it was in the protostellar phase (before nuclear fusion in the core started). In the future, helium will continue to accumulate in the core, and in about 5 billion years this gradual build-up will eventually cause the Sun to exit the main sequence and become a red giant.[51]

The chemical composition of the photosphere is normally considered representative of the composition of the primordial Solar System.[52] The solar heavy-element abundances described above are typically measured both using spectroscopy of the Sun's photosphere and by measuring abundances in meteorites that have never been heated to melting temperatures. These meteorites are thought to retain the composition of the protostellar Sun and are thus not affected by the settling of heavy elements. The two methods generally agree well.

The CORE

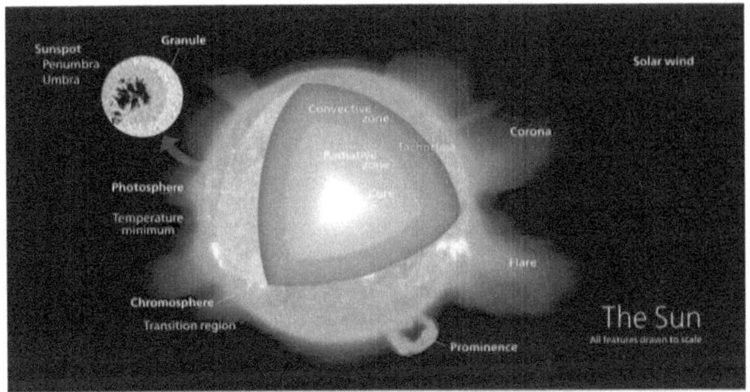

Illustration of the Sun's structure, in false color for contrast

Enter Caption

The core of the Sun extends from the center to about 20–25% of the solar radius.[53] It has a density of up to 150 g/cm3[54][55] (about 150 times the density of water) and a temperature of close to 15.7 million kelvins (K).[55] By contrast, the Sun's surface temperature is approximately 5800 K. Recent analysis of SOHO mission data favors a faster rotation rate in the core than in the radiative zone above.[53] Through most of the Sun's life, energy has been produced by nuclear fusion in the core region through the proton–proton chain; this process converts hydrogen into helium.[56] Currently, only 0.8% of the energy generated in the Sun comes from another sequence of fusion reactions called the CNO cycle, though this proportion is expected to increase as the Sun becomes older and more luminous.[57][58]

The core is the only region in the Sun that produces an appreciable amount of thermal energy through fusion; 99% of the power is generated within 24% of the Sun's radius, and by 30% of the radius, fusion has stopped nearly entirely. The remainder of the Sun is heated by this energy as it is transferred outwards through many successive layers, finally to the solar photosphere where it escapes into space through radiation (photons) or advection (massive particles).

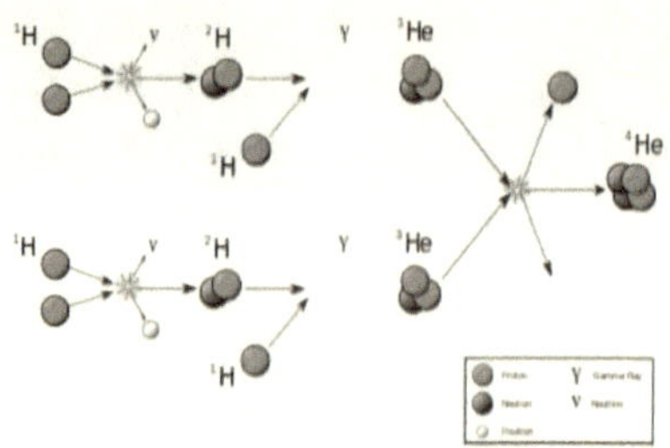

Illustration of a proton-proton reaction chain, from hydrogen forming deuterium, helium-3, and regular helium-4.

Enter Caption

The proton–proton chain occurs around 9.2×10^{37} times each second in the core, converting about 3.7×10^{38} protons into alpha particles (helium nuclei) every second (out of a total of $\sim8.9\times10^{56}$ free protons in the Sun), or about 6.2×10^{11} kg/s. However, each proton (on average) takes around 9 billion years to fuse with one another using the PP chain.[59] Fusing four free protons (hydrogen nuclei) into a single alpha particle (helium nucleus) releases around 0.7% of the fused mass as energy,[61] so the Sun releases energy at the mass–energy conversion rate of 4.26 million metric tons per second (which requires 600 metric megatons of hydrogen[62]), for 384.6 yottawatts (3.846×1026 W),[5] or 9.192×1010 megatons of TNT per second. The large power output of the Sun is mainly due to the huge size and density of its core (compared to Earth and objects on Earth), with only a fairly small amount of power being generated per cubic metre. Theoretical models of the Sun's interior indicate a maximum power density, or energy production, of approximately 276.5 watts per cubic metre at the center of the core,[63] which is about the same power density inside a compost pile.[64][e]

The fusion rate in the core is in a self-correcting equilibrium: a slightly higher rate of fusion would cause the core to heat up more and expand slightly against the weight of the outer layers, reducing the density and hence the fusion rate and correcting the perturbation; and a slightly lower rate would cause the core to cool and shrink slightly, increasing the density and increasing the fusion rate and again reverting it to its present rate.

The Earth

Earth is the third planet from the Sun and the only astronomical object known to harbor life. While large volumes of water can be found throughout the Solar System, only Earth sustains liquid surface water. About 71% of Earth's surface is made up of the ocean, dwarfing Earth's polar ice, lakes, and rivers. The remaining 29% of Earth's surface is land, consisting of continents and islands. Earth's surface layer is formed of several slowly moving tectonic plates, interacting to produce mountain ranges, volcanoes, and earthquakes. Earth's liquid outer core generates the magnetic field that shapes Earth's magnetosphere, deflecting destructive solar winds.

Earth's atmosphere consists mostly of nitrogen and oxygen. More solar energy is received by tropical regions than polar regions and is redistributed by atmospheric and ocean circulation. Water vapor is widely present in the atmosphere and forms clouds that cover most of the planet. Greenhouse gases in the atmosphere like carbon dioxide (CO_2) trap a part of the energy from the Sun close to the surface. A region's climate is governed by latitude, but also by elevation and proximity to moderating oceans. Severe weather, such as tropical cyclones, thunderstorms, and heatwaves, occurs in most areas and greatly impacts life.

Earth is an ellipsoid with a circumference of about 40,000 km. It is the densest planet in the Solar System. Of the four rocky planets, it is the largest and most massive. Earth is about eight light minutes away from the Sun and orbits it, taking a year (about 365.25 days) to complete one revolution. Earth rotates around its own axis in slightly less than a day (in about 23 hours and 56 minutes). Earth's axis of rotation is tilted with respect to the perpendicular to its orbital plane around the Sun, producing seasons. Earth is orbited by one permanent natural satellite, the Moon, which orbits Earth at 380,000 km (1.3 light seconds) and is roughly a quarter as wide as Earth. The Moon always faces the Earth with the same side through tidal locking and causes tides, stabilizes Earth's axis, and gradually slows its rotation.

Earth formed over 4.5 billion years ago. During the first billion years of Earth's history, the ocean formed and then life developed within it. Life spread globally and began to affect Earth's atmosphere and surface, leading to Earth's Great Oxidation Event two billion years ago. Humans emerged 300,000 years ago, and have reached a population of almost 8 billion today. Humans depend on Earth's biosphere and natural resources for their survival, but have increasingly impacted Earth's environment. Today, humanity's impact on Earth's climate, soils, waters, and ecosystems is unsustainable, threatening people's lives and causing widespread extinction of other life.

Enter Caption

Etimology

The modern English word Earth developed, via Middle English, from an Old English noun most often spelled eorðe.[26] It has cognates in every Germanic language, and their ancestral root has been reconstructed as *erþō. In its earliest attestation, the word eorðe was already being used to translate the many senses of Latin terra and Greek γῆ gē: the ground, its soil, dry land, the human world, the surface of the world (including the sea), and the globe itself. As with Roman Terra/Tellūs and Greek Gaia, Earth may have been a personified goddess in Germanic paganism: late Norse mythology included Jörð ('Earth'), a giantess often given as the mother of Thor.[27]

Historically, earth has been written in lowercase. From early Middle English, its definite sense as "the globe" was expressed as the earth. By Early Modern English, many nouns were capitalized, and the earth was also written the Earth, particularly when referenced along with other heavenly bodies. More recently, the name is sometimes simply given as Earth, by analogy with the names of the other planets, though earth and forms with the remain common.[26] House styles now vary: Oxford spelling recognizes the lowercase form as the most common, with the capitalized form an acceptable variant. Another convention capitalizes "Earth" when appearing as a name (for example, "Earth's atmosphere") but writes it in lowercase when preceded by the (for example, "the atmosphere of the earth"). It almost always appears in lowercase in colloquial expressions such as "what on earth are you doing?"[28]

Occasionally, the name Terra /ˈtɛrə/ is used in scientific writing and especially in science fiction to distinguish humanity's inhabited planet from others,[29] while in poetry Tellus /ˈtɛləs/ has been used to denote personification of the Earth.[30] Terra is also the name of the planet in some Romance languages (languages that evolved from Latin) like Italian and Portuguese, while in other Romance languages the word gave rise to names with slightly altered spellings (like the Spanish Tierra and the French Terre). The Latinate form Gæa or Gaea (English: /ˈdʒiː.ə/) of the Greek poetic name Gaia (Γαῖα; Ancient Greek: [gâi̯.a] or [gâj.ja]) is rare, though the alternative spelling Gaia has become common due to the Gaia hypothesis, in which case its pronunciation is /ˈgaɪ.ə/ rather than the more classical English /ˈgeɪ.ə/.[31]

There are a number of adjectives for the planet Earth. From Earth itself comes earthly. From the Latin Terra comes terran /ˈtɛrən/,[32] terrestrial /təˈrɛstriəl/,[33] and (via French) terrene /təˈriːn/,[34] and from the Latin Tellus comes tellurian /tɛˈlʊəriən/[35] and telluric.

Formation

The oldest material found in the Solar System is dated to 4.5682+0.0002

−0.0004 Ga (billion years) ago.[37] By 4.54±0.04 Ga the primordial Earth had formed.[38] The bodies in the Solar System formed and evolved with the Sun. In theory, a solar nebula partitions a volume out of a molecular cloud by gravitational collapse, which begins to spin and flatten into a circumstellar disk, and then the planets grow out of that disk with the Sun. A nebula contains gas, ice grains, and dust (including primordial nuclides). According to nebular theory, planetesimals formed by accretion, with the primordial Earth being estimated as likely taking anywhere from 70 to 100 million years to form.[39]

Estimates of the age of the Moon range from 4.5 Ga to significantly younger.[40] A leading hypothesis is that it was formed by accretion from material loosed from Earth after a Mars-sized object with about 10% of Earth's mass, named Theia, collided with Earth.[41] It hit Earth with a glancing blow and some of its mass merged with Earth.[42][43] Between approximately 4.1 and 3.8 Ga, numerous asteroid impacts during the Late Heavy Bombardment caused significant changes to the greater surface environment of the Moon and, by inference, to that of Earth.

Origin of Life and Evolution

Chemical reactions led to the first self-replicating molecules about four billion years ago. A half billion years later, the last common ancestor of all current life arose.[61] The evolution of photosynthesis allowed the Sun's energy to be harvested directly by life forms. The resultant molecular oxygen ($O2$) accumulated in the atmosphere and due to interaction with ultraviolet solar radiation, formed a protective ozone layer ($O3$) in the upper atmosphere.[62] The incorporation of smaller cells within larger ones resulted in the development of complex cells called eukaryotes.[63] True multicellular organisms formed as cells within colonies became increasingly specialized. Aided by the absorption of harmful ultraviolet radiation by the ozone layer, life colonized Earth's surface.[64] Among the earliest fossil evidence for life is microbial mat fossils found in 3.48 billion-year-old sandstone in Western Australia,[65] biogenic graphite found in 3.7 billion-year-old metasedimentary rocks in Western Greenland,[66] and remains of biotic material found in 4.1 billion-year-old rocks in Western Australia.[67][68] The earliest direct evidence of life on Earth is contained in 3.45 billion-year-old Australian rocks showing fossils of microorganisms.[69][70]

During the Neoproterozoic, 1000 to 539 Ma, much of Earth might have been covered in ice. This hypothesis has been termed "Snowball Earth", and it is of particular interest because it preceded the Cambrian explosion, when multicellular life forms significantly increased in complexity.[71][72] Following the Cambrian explosion, 535 Ma, there have been at least five major mass extinctions and many minor ones.[73][74] Apart from the proposed current Holocene extinction event, the most recent was 66 Ma, when an asteroid impact triggered the extinction of the non-avian dinosaurs and other large reptiles, but largely spared small animals such as insects, mammals, lizards and birds. Mammalian life has diversified over the past 66 Mys, and several million years ago an African ape gained the ability to stand upright.[75] This facilitated tool use and encouraged communication that provided the nutrition and stimulation needed for a larger brain, which led to the evolution of humans. The development of agriculture, and then civilization, led to humans having an influence on Earth and the nature and quantity of other life forms that continues to this day.